TIME SPACE AND DRUMS PART SEVEN

ACCENTS
DRUMMING
Development

TIME SPACE AND DRUMS PART SEVEN

ACCENTS
DRUMMING
Development

BIG BANGS & EXPLOSIONS

The Time Space & Drums Series
A Complete Program of Lessons in Professional, Contemporary Rock, and Jazz Drumming Styles.

Written and Developed By:
Stephen Hawkins

Graphic Design By: Nathaniel Dasco.
Special Thanks To Linda Drouin and Ikhide Oshoma

ThinkeLife Publications

Time Space and Drums Copyright 2021 By Stephen Hawkins.

All Rights Reserved.

No part of this book may be reproduced in any form or by any electronic or mechanical means including information storage and retrieval means without permission in writing from the author.

The only exception is by a reviewer, who may quote short excerpts in a review.

Stephen Hawkins – Time Space and Drums
Visit my website at www.timespaceanddrums.com

First printing: Jan 2021.

ISBN: 978 1 913929 06 0

Dedicated to the late Paul Daniels and family, Martin Daniels, Trevor Daniels, Paul Mellor's, Keith Richards, Peter Windle, Andrew Marple's, Colin Keys, Peters & Lee, Susan Maughan, Ronnie Dukes, Tom O'Connor, Les Dennis, the late Bob Monkhouse, Bobby Davro, Tommy Bruce, Robert Young, Sandie Gold as well as the hundreds of other people who have played a part in my life experience. Including Sphinx Entertainment, E & B Productions as well as the hundreds of fantastic personalities I have had the pleasure of working alongside over the past 35 years. Apologies for anyone I have missed, not forgetting the current reader who I hope will receive as much from their drumming as I have and more – Stephen Hawkins.

Table of Contents

DRUM ROLL, PLEASE! 1

INTRODUCTION 1

Lesson 1: 1/8th Note Accents in 2/4 Time 7

Lesson 2: Accents in 2/4, 3/4, and 4/4 Time Using Alternate Sticking 9

Lesson 3: 1/8th Note & 1/16th Note Accents in 5/4 and 7/4 Time 15

Lesson 4: Triplet Accents in 3/8, 2/4, 3/4, 4/4, and 5/4 Time 19

    Big Bangs & Explosions 23

    RUDIMENTARY 25

  Recapitulation 25

  The Buzz Roll 25

    Featured Drummer Recommendations 27

  Conclusion 29

DRUM ROLL, PLEASE!

INTRODUCTION

If you have been following the Time Space and Drums Series from the beginning then congratulations are in order for making it this far. You should by now be well on your way to creating a fantastic foundational base to work from. Even though we are beginning to develop in different areas, this is all still part of the foundation.

You should now also be aware of your weak points in relation to what we have covered so far in previous books within the series. You should begin to work on these weaknesses right now, before continuing with this book, in order to bring everything up to scratch.

When you are completely satisfied that your weak points have become as strong as your strongest points or well on their way to becoming strong points, then you should continue with this set of four lessons.

However, should you need any work done on your left-hand, your bass drum, or any other aspect of your starting technique, you should work on that aspect until the problem has been solved.

Again, when you're happy, you can carry on.

We are now going to start to develop your musicianship by developing your rudimentary skills further. Namely—playing accents with either hand on the snare drum.

You should first begin by making absolutely sure that you are getting the very best out of your equipment.

That is:

1) Make sure that you are getting the very best out of your drums by tuning them regularly. Ensure that you like what you hear when you strike the drums. If not, then work on this over the coming weeks and months. Make it a primary concern every time you enter a practice session. Simply become aware of how your drums sound and attempt to quickly render the issues that you encounter. But do not, under any circumstances, avoid your actual practice session because you are unhappy with your sound.

2) Double-check that your equipment is setup for maximum impact and playability. Check the position of your snare drum. Is it at the right angle? is it too near or too far away from you when you play? The same thing goes for the toms and cymbals. Make sure neither is too far away or too near and at the right angles to you, and you can play every instrument without stretching. In short, make sure everything is within easy reach. If you're not 100% happy with anything then do something about it until you are.

By tuning and positioning your equipment correctly, you will get more enjoyment out of playing the drums. It will also be much easier to play them, especially for longer periods of time.

Having done all of this and made ourselves aware of potential tuning and setup issues, let's move on to the next set of lessons. As usual, take them at a sensible pace, and don't be too eager to finish. These are a very valuable part of your drumming foundational skills. They will also help develop your dynamic creativity more as you perfect them. For example, you can give a basic $1/16^{th}$ note drum fill a big boost by accenting certain notes. Your overall dynamics will also improve. If you are a gigging drummer, you will begin to notice that when you play on gigs that the more dynamic playing begins to show without thinking about it. In this, drumming is really all about programming the techniques beats, and rhythms into your mind.

So, what is an accent? An accent is any note that is played louder than the majority of the notes in a particular beat or piece of music. On the other side of the scale, we have ghost notes. A ghost note is any note played quieter than the majority of the notes in a particular beat or piece of music. So now we understand what an accent is, let's take a deeper look at this particular book's main ideas, purpose and concepts.

I will briefly recap the book description and contents then give some underlying advice and tips. I will also highlight basic information about the intention of the particular set of lessons plus other useful information you can make use of as your drumming develops.

The Time Space and Drums' Accents Drumming Development Course includes only four drumming lessons. These lessons are designed to take the complete beginner through a process that builds dynamics into the drummer's arsenal of techniques and abilities.

As well as learning how to add dynamics to the student's skill set, this course of drumming lessons also covers playing accents in a variety of time signatures including 2/4,

3/4, 4/4, 5/4, and more. As a result, the student will emerge with a fully rounded and dynamic accent playing ability, as well as improved odd-time playing skills.

All advanced dynamic drumming concepts are built on these vital fundamental skills. Therefore, this seventh book in the series further develops the drumming foundation skills already covered through the series so far and begins to give the drummers' present abilities a dynamic boost.

These building blocks begin to take the drummer's current skills to the next level of development as the drummer begins to sound much more comfortable and competent at the drum set.

I will briefly give an example of what this set of lessons can do for your playing. But first, may I add that there are many great drummers out there. They play reasonably great time and an array of reasonably complex stuff. However, in only one or two videos out of a hundred that I have watched have I ever seen, since Dave Weckl brought us the power stroke, another drummer who plays great dynamics within his/her playing. They all seem to play rhythmically brilliantly with very little dynamics within their playing, unless it's a straight move from playing loud to playing medium loud to playing softly. Then back to loud again. There are generally no in-betweens.

And so, let me give you a brief example of what adding dynamics can do to your playing.

Here's the example, which is taken from the Rock Drumming Foundation Course Essence email. It is first sung in a scientific way all at one level or volume, and then sung again more dynamically.

www.timespaceanddrums.com/audio/Dynamic.mp3

I will describe what is happening here through the use of a more complex example. On the surface, it seems that I am playing or rather singing, let's say 32 x $1/16^{th}$ notes as an example, all at varying volumes. Giving the appearance of what we are calling dynamic playing.

But that's not what is happening at all.

What is happening is that the time is being moved and shifted into various places in advance. It is behind the beat in such a way that the time remains solid and straight but is being bent by the drummer's interpretation of the pulse. All the time, it is pushing that pulse forward to convey the time or meter.

Because this is not a mathematical equation, it is ridiculously complicated and difficult for me to describe exactly. Dave Weckl describes the power stroke then later describes the ghost notes before moving on to describe playing backward, either 1/8th or 1/16th in front or behind the beat... This is as close as I can describe what is occurring in dynamic playing in a purely mathematical way.

Putting it mathematically, it would best be described as playing backward and forwards using power stokes and ghost notes in a random fashion by displacing the place where you "think" <u>on</u> the beat.

It is the feel of the thing that you play. But as you play it, you are systematically moving the one: you displace it, and then shift it again.

And yes, I know that makes absolutely no sense at all but it is the best and most succinctly that I can say it.

If you imagine a continuous pulse then sing 1/16th notes as I just did, you will be able to see what I mean if you look with your mind at the sounds being played in relation to the actual pulse. But bear in mind that the pulse is silent and not really evident.

There would be many what you might call mistakes of judgment that I would make if I had opted to sing a more complex example than the basic rock beat in the above audio demonstration. However, because I have a good foundation of playing the basics of time, the mistakes are quickly rectified. They are then tied to the next note that was played on time or was molded on the spot into a rhythm that came back into focus in regards to the pulse. I see this more as predicting what is being played and what will be played next in quick succession so that it appears to be played smoothly, flowingly, and dynamically.

But please... if all of what I just said makes absolutely no sense to you, do not worry about it. You will discover this for yourself after you have gained some control over the exercises in this book and developed more as a drummer. This will occur especially when you develop more dynamically. In short, this is simply weaving up and down in volume and playing around the pulse of the beat or music.

During the development of this little book, I could have filled a 100-page book of accent exercises but thought it best to limit the exercises so as to allow the student drummer to gain better control of the ones I did include here. This, like many areas of drumming, is a concept that grows without end from these first beginning examples and exercises. It is then up to the individual student drummer to print out pages of $1/8^{th}$ and/or $1/16^{th}$ notes and then grab a pen, then start marking accents at various places above the notes to give a vast, even unlimited number of accent combinations for him or herself to practice. But as I said, the exercises in this book will go a very long way to allowing your current drumming skills to more easily shine through by the use of dynamics within your playing.

However, hat isn't to say that you play these exercises as they are in your general playing. As suggested earlier, you will begin to notice that you automatically, in most cases, begin to play everything in a more dynamic way. When that happens, you will begin to understand everything I said earlier about displacing and bending time itself.

Well, that about covers the introduction to dynamic playing, so let me leave you with a valuable tip.

This whole playing dynamically is really born from, or put another way... the center of gravity for all of this dynamic playing is playing what I call *"prettily"*. I prefer the word *prettily* to describe what I am getting at due to the high-quality sound of the cymbals tied in with the perfectly tuned drums. When they are hitting the drums gently or very softly, the sound is what I call *pretty*.

Within the *pretty*, light playing, there are slight nuances and dynamics going on.

Then when you play power strokes, make it thunder or anything in-between, the playing takes on a new level. The drummer then begins to sound as if he is playing complex rhythms when all he is doing is playing a string of $1/16^{th}$ notes or maybe triplets. He is maybe mixing $1/16^{th}$ notes and triples dynamically and from the central gravity point of playing *pretty*.

And so, when you begin to add flams after all of that, the drummer begins to sound like a complete pro, intermediate, or even advanced player.

But bear in mind that I see a drum or cymbal as having its own unique and individual sound and should be respected for that; it should not be thrashed as if it were a dustbin lid. This is the main reason I am not partial to most forms of rock music, especially the heavy rock types. But that's just my personal preference.

As I originally stated in the description of the Time Space and Drums Rock Drumming Foundation... It's not what you do, it's the way that you do it. Here you take on another level of mastery as you respect the drum as you hit for what it does and how it sounds. The same thing applies to the cymbals.

So, keep practicing and have fun playing your pretty little heart out. Seriously, it's fun and sounds great when you have tuned your drum to sound great.

Until next time…

Let's strike those skins. *(prettily of course?)*

Stephen J. Hawkins

Free Audio Demonstrations

You should visit the following URL to download audio demonstrations of every exercise in this book as soon as possible. You will then receive additional tips and guidance through the included essence emails.

www.timespaceanddrums.com/tsd-7acc.html

Lesson 1

1/8th Note Accents in 2/4 Time

The first part of lesson 1 will cover accents in 2/4 and 4/4 time using 1/8th and 1/16th notes. Be sure to perfect the single-hand accents described in exercises 1-4 and 2-8 before going further. This will get your individual hands used to playing accented notes.

Exercises 1-8

Exercises 1-4 are RH accents while exercises 5-8 are LH accent exercises. Play each bar several times before going on to the next bar. I have written these exercises in groups of 4 bars. The timing is 2/4 or 4 1/8th notes per bar. When you have practiced and perfected each bar, you may then practice exercises 1-4 as a 4-bar phrase.

Exercises 1-4

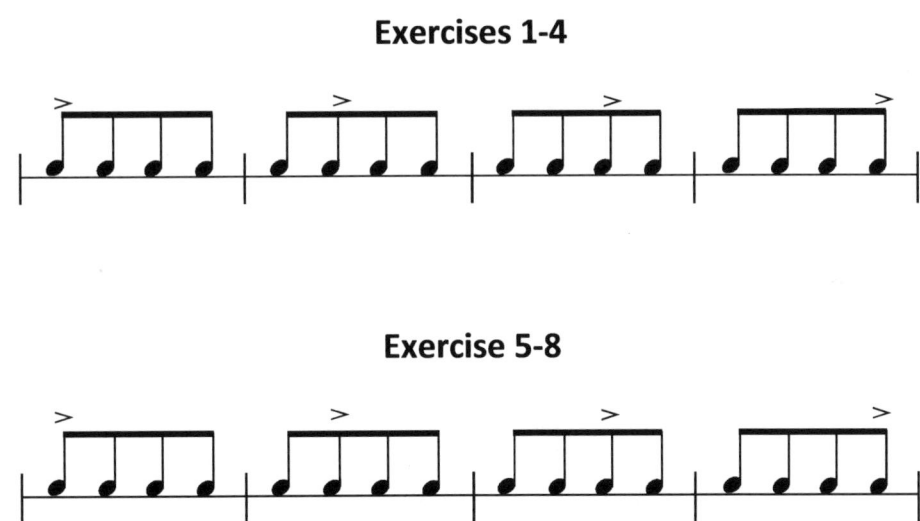

Exercise 5-8

When you can play these two sets of exercises with both hands individually, you may then continue, playing 1 bar at a time and repeating it until it is perfect using alternate sticking. Move on to the next bar and so on, then again play the 4-bar phrase a few times.

Exercises 9-26

This next set of exercises are all RIGHT-HANDED Exercises. Begin slowly and build the strength in your RH. When you can play them easily and in perfect time, move on to the next set of LH exercises.

Time Space and Drums — Big Bangs & Explosions

Exercise 27-44

Now try these LEFT-HANDED Exercises. Again, start slowly and build the strength in your LH

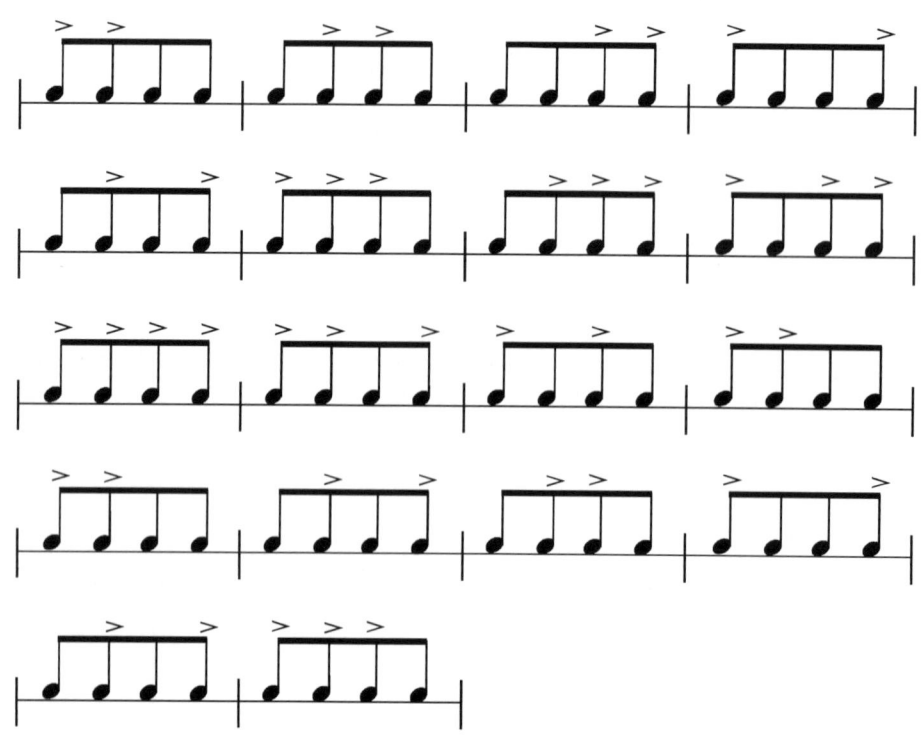

Lesson 2

1/8th Note & 1/16th Note Accents in 2/4, 3/4, and 4/4 Time

Using Alternate Sticking

Exercise 1-22

The following exercises are to be played with alternate sticking.

Time Space and Drums   Big Bangs & Explosions

As you can see, so far, we have covered playing accents with the RH followed by the same exercises playing with your LH. You should try and do this with every set of exercises.

Exercise 23-42

Use alternate sticking for these exercises and remember to practice each bar 1 at a time before practicing them as 4-bar phrases.

Again, you can get creative here and practice these exercises with the RH, then with the LH. You can do this with just 1 bar at a time, 2 bars at a time, 4 bars at a time, or playing through the set of exercises before changing hands. But don't forget to practice them using alternate sticking too.

Stephen Hawkins

Time Space and Drums   Big Bangs & Explosions

This will really develop the strength in your wrists and fingers. When you finish these exercise sets, you will be surprised how much they help you play everything else much better with more precision and accuracy.

Exercise 43-62

Now let's practice some exercises in 3/4-time, 1 bar at a time.

Again, do what you have done before. Play a single bar and practice that, then 2 bars followed by 4 bars followed by the whole set of exercises with each hand individually and then both hands alternately.

Exercise 63-80

This time, use these 1/16th note accents one bar at a time.

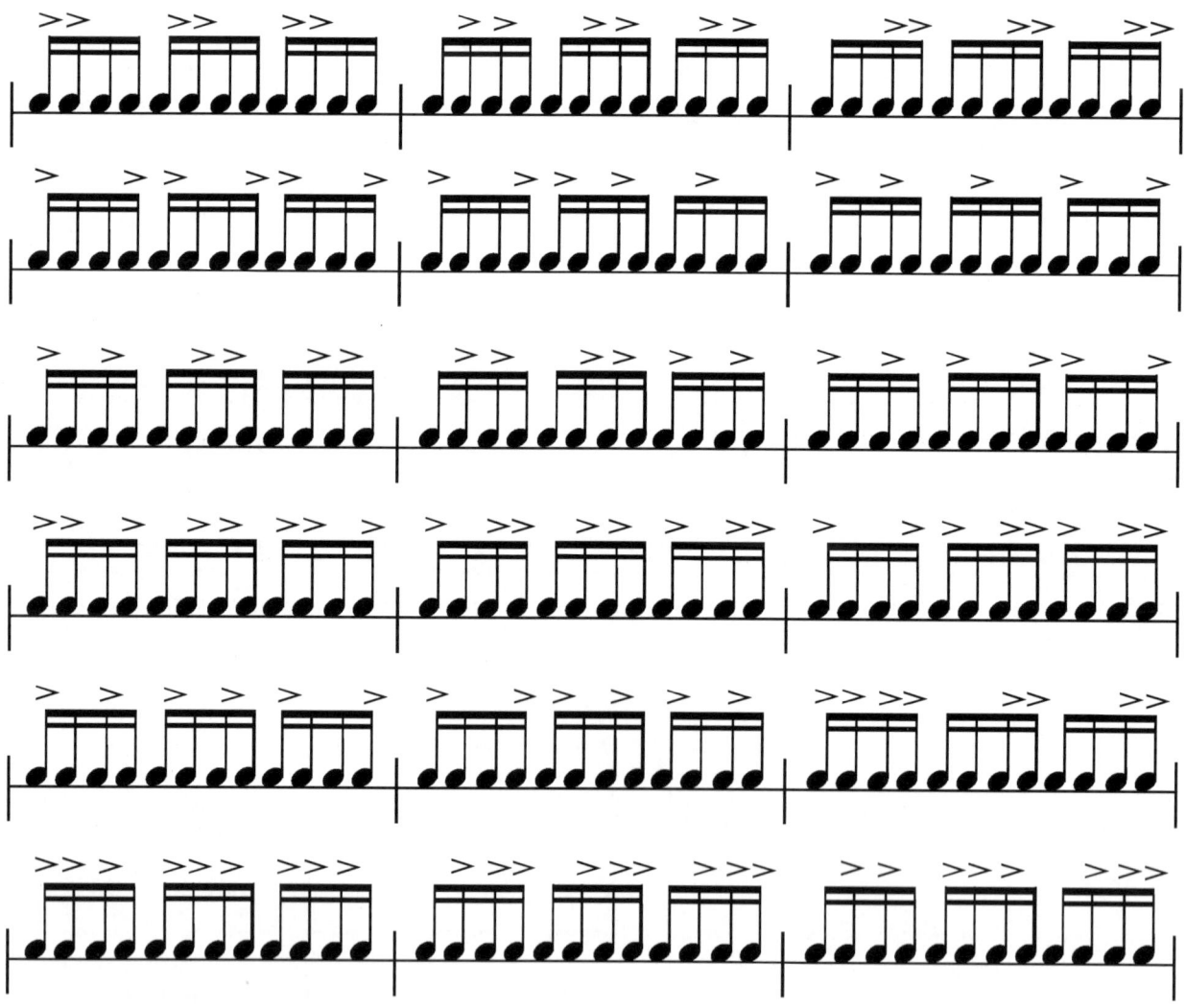

You can practice this set in the same manner as before but begin practicing slower to make sure that you can keep up.

As you get more and more used to playing these accent exercises with each hand individually, you will become aware of a constant flog movement that needs to be maintained as you play the accents. You will understand this more as you get better at playing these exercises. It's sort of like a rocking motion when you play the accents versus when you play ghost notes.

Exercise 81-92

Now for some 4/4 accented exercises, 1 bar at a time.

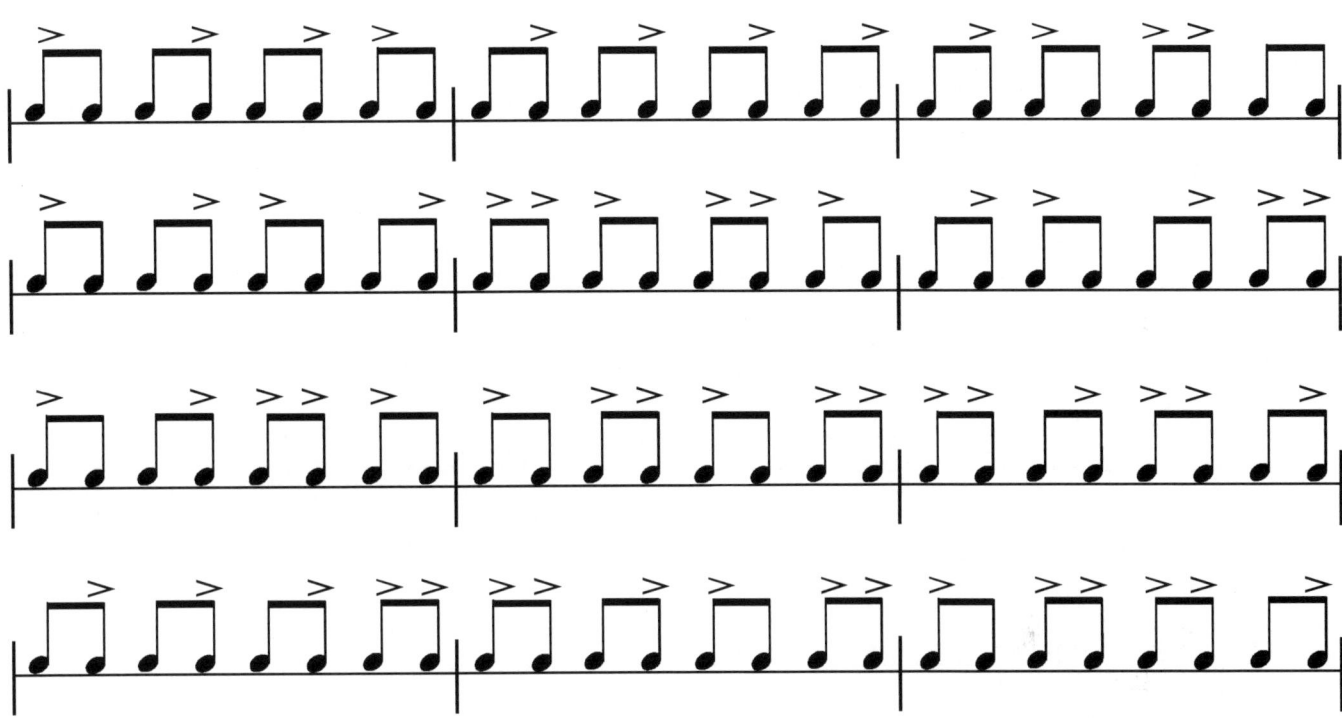

It would be a good idea at this point to try playing a 3 bars rock style beat; you can choose any of the 6 we covered in part one and then play 1 bar from the above exercise set at a time. Play them as they are using alternate sticking exercises on the snare drum. You can add the bass drum and hi-hats to the fill to keep the pulse.

Alternatively, you can again play 3 bars 4/4 rock style beat then practice the above exercises as drum fills by playing the accents on the tom-toms. You can simply move the accented note onto the hi-tom, mid-tom, or low-tom, depending on the accent position and your ability to use various toms instead of just playing on a single one. But that's okay too.

Since this is a new way to play the exercises, you may want to go back to the beginning of this book and begin practicing the exercises by playing the accents on tom-toms. BUT be

Time Space and Drums — Big Bangs & Explosions

aware that these are to be mastered as far as possible just on the snare drum. I am merely giving you a few ideas to approach these exercises.

Exercise 93-104

Use 1/16th notes this time, then practice them as 2-bar phrases.

Even though these are 1/16th note exercises, you can still try playing the accents on the tom-toms using alternative sticking. This will begin to strengthen your arms in regard to moving around the kit and playing the toms in drum-fills, etc. But again, master these on the snare drum only first.

Lesson 3

1/8th Note & 1/16th Note Accents in 5/4 and 7/4 Time

Exercise 1-12

This time, we will use 1/8th notes in 5/4 time. Practice them 1 bar at a time and then as 2-bar phrases.

Exercise 13-26

This time, we'll use 1/16th notes. Play 1 bar at a time then again as 2-bar phrases.

Exercise 27-34

Now for some 7/4 1/8th note accents.

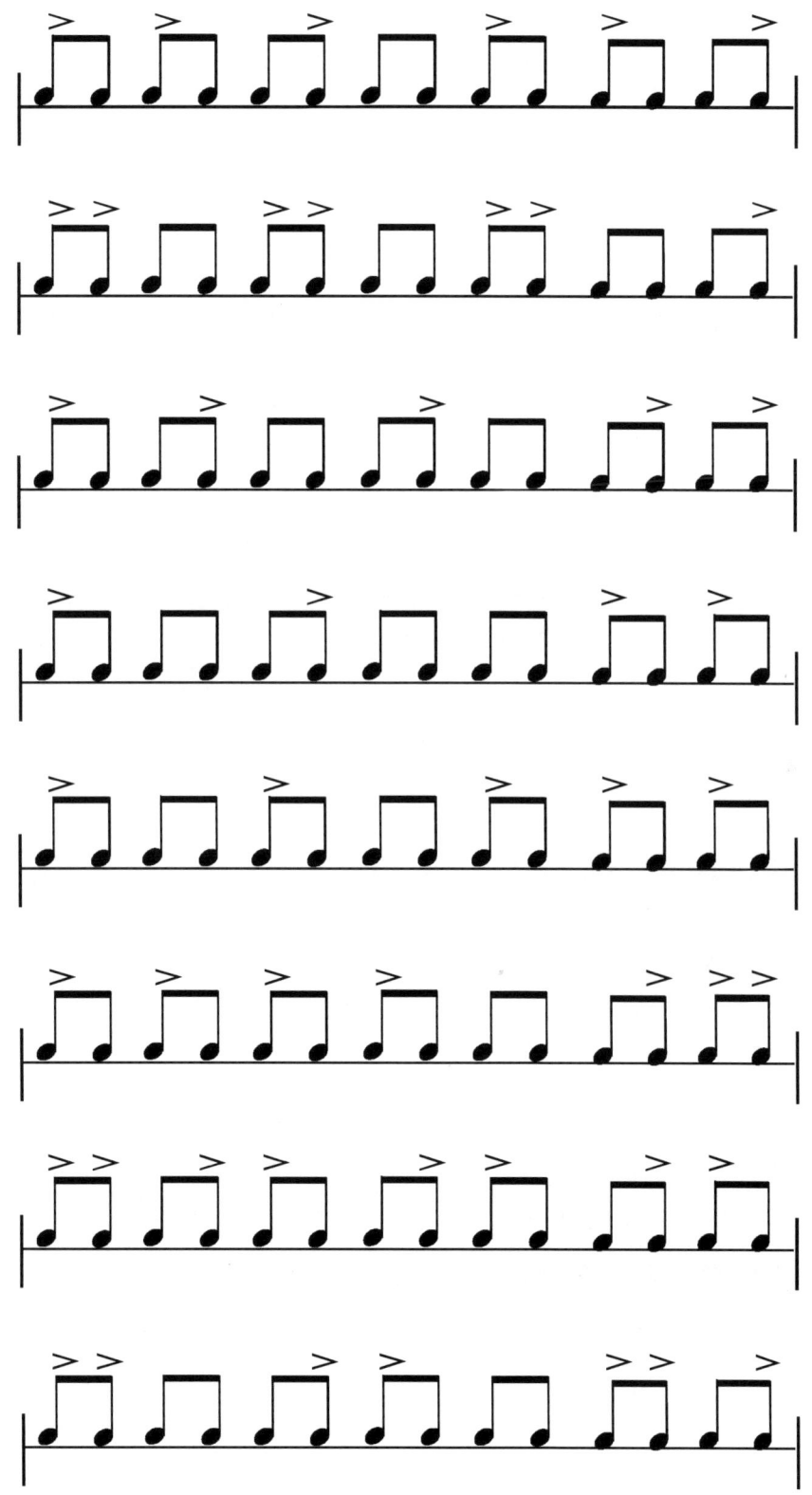

Exercise 35-38

Now we'll use 1/16th notes in 7/4 time.

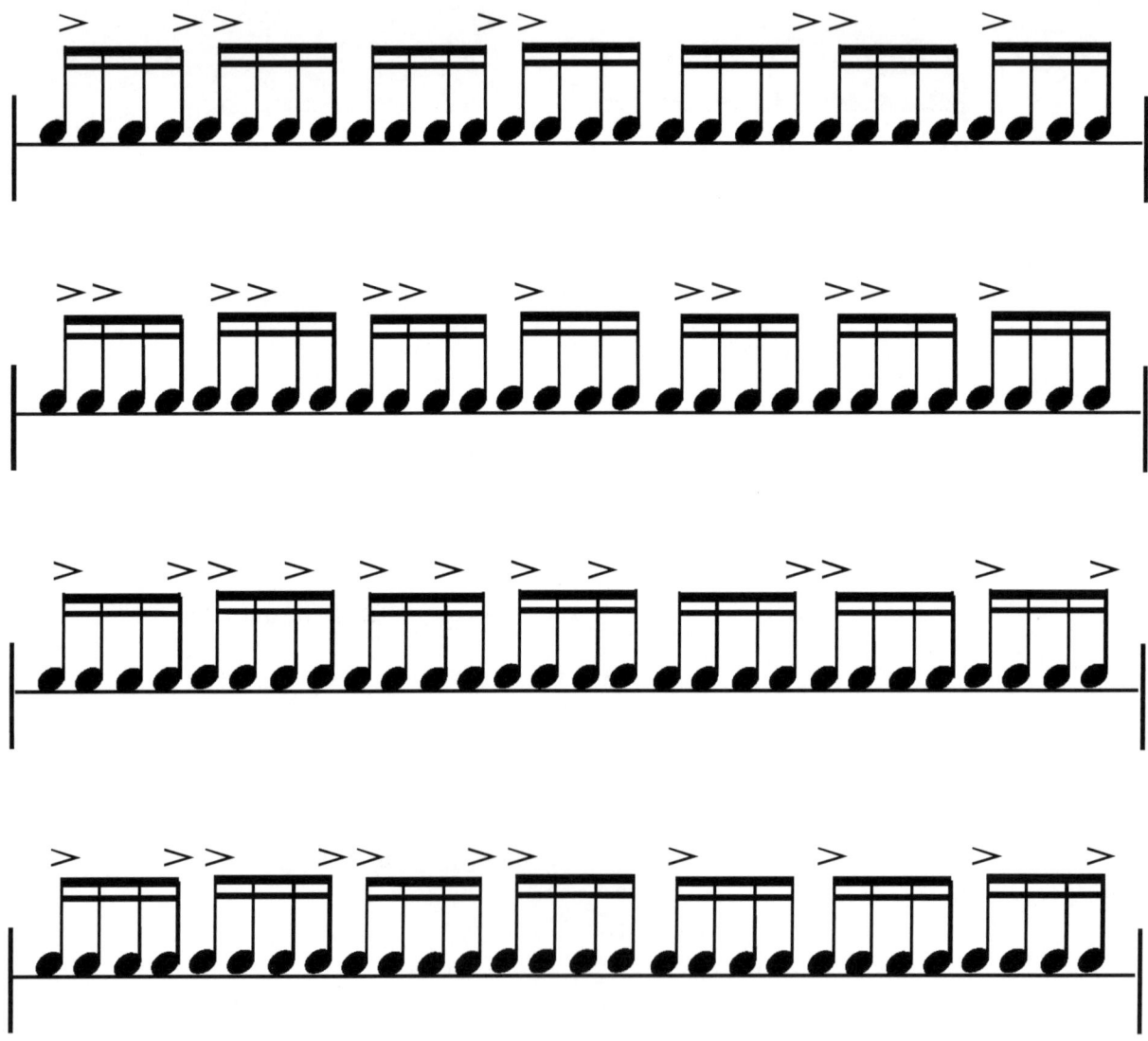

And again, what goes for 4/4, you can also practice in 5/4. Try playing the toms on the accented notes, then try playing phrases of 4 bars by playing one of the bars from the previous 5/4 and 7/4 exercises above as a drum fill.

Lesson 4

Triplet Accents in 3/8, 2/4, 3/4, 4/4 and 5/4 Time

Exercise 1-6

Exercise 7-12

Exercise 13-18

Although the above exercises and a few to follow are just single or double sets of triplets, as in 3/8 or 2/4,, you can still try playing them as 4-bar phrased drum fills. You can do this by playing 3 bars of a swing, 12/8, or shuffle beat then playing these accented triplets as they are on the snare drum or a drum fill. Play the accented notes on the tom-toms.

You can even begin to play the accented notes, along with the bass drum, using the crash cymbals to form little phrases over a single bar. Next, get straight back into the beat you were playing for another 3 bars then choose a different drum fill from the exercises here and play your phrase, and so on.

Try a variety of ways if you can think of them and don't be afraid to make mistakes whilst you try new things. But having said that, please note it is important to acknowledge that you have made a mistake and then try to correct it next time around.

Exercise 19-42

This time we'll play triplet exercises in 2/4 time.

Exercise 43-54

Now for some triplet accents in 3/4 time.

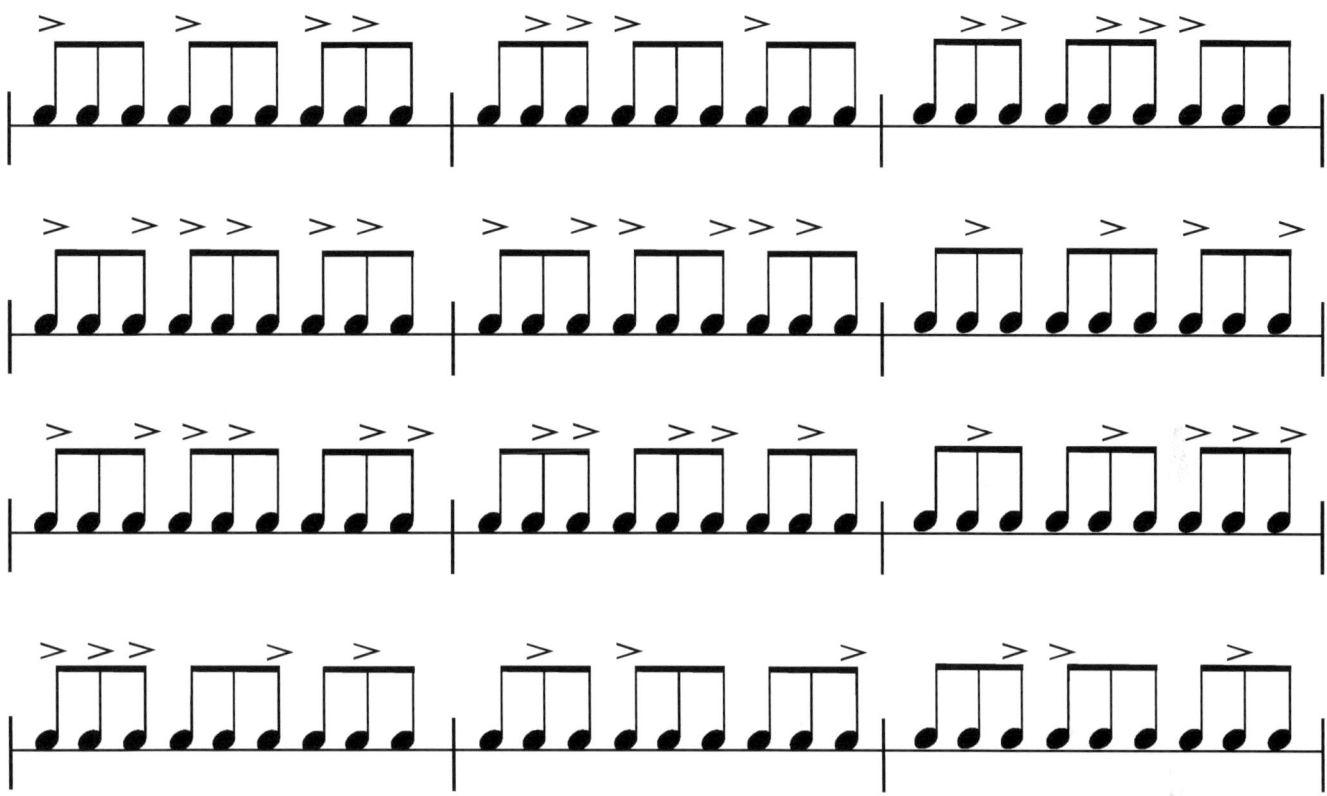

Going back to my previous remark about making mistakes, you can't really make a mistake whilst you are learning something. When you start practicing what you have learned, well, that's another matter; you should always recognize a mistake and remove it as soon as possible so as not to become great at making many of them.

Become great at playing the exercises and the other things; practice a lot and one day you will become great.

Exercise 55-66

Now let's try some 4/4 exercises.

Exercise 67-78

Now we'll try some exercises in 5/4 time.

Big Bangs & Explosions

Again, the title Big Bangs & Explosions is a metaphor for the dynamics within drumming.

But herein lies the possibility of completely messing up the dynamics simply because there is no central point from which those dynamics are born. In other words, what defines loud and quiet, and everything in between, above and below those distinctions?

Well, the first place to look is the physical environment or space where the drumming is taking place, in an attempt to view any obstacle that would interfere with the dynamics of the sound such as materials and furnishings. If, for example, you are playing in a wooden room, the sound of the drums would be quite loud and openly ringing. Therefore, a gentle tap would produce the same sound as a much harder tap in a room full of curtains.

These considerations will help a little but the dynamic range really comes from the drummer. If you generally play pretty hard then anything louder than that would be very difficult, if not impossible. There would be no room for louder dynamics in your playing. If, on the other hand, you were a gentle hitter then there wouldn't be anywhere to go as far as softer hits and ghost notes.

I was often asked if I was a rock drummer whenever I played with a rock band; however, I did not like it because, from my perspective, there is nowhere else to go if everything you do is hard rock. It categorizes you as a hard hitter and therefore limits you in the dynamic ranges possible, so I prefer to begin from a central point of reference where I can go much quieter or much louder. The difference or range is then quite big.

If you're a heavy hitter, on the other hand, who can quieten down a little, or a lot, it always requires you to get back up to that hard-hitting which I personally am not a fan of. I prefer the dynamic ups and downs rather than the dynamic downs then back up again.

You may be different and that's fine too but remember it's always nice to be able to add the power when the music requires it rather than have the power on all of the time, even when the music doesn't require it. That's not a good place to be and I am sure you can adjust to suit your situation.

However, all of this is going off-topic slightly; the aim of these exercises is to develop accents from a central point of reference. You can then play ghost notes as well as accented power strokes. You will then find yourself suddenly adding dynamics to your drumming as opposed to being constantly at one volume all of the time, which can get quite monotonous.

The Big Bang theory itself regarding sound is really a misnomer because, if there was a big bang (bang referring to loud noise), then no one would have heard a sound due to lack of gravity. Therefore, there was nothing to carry the sound, so any noise or bang would have been silent.

But for practical purposes, the big bang really serves as a reference point regarding the starting point or central point of the dynamic range which allows for much harder as well as much quieter sounds.

RUDIMENTARY

Recapitulation

So far, we have covered:

- The Single Stroke Roll in Book 1,
- Single Stroke Triplets in Book 2,
- The Double Stroke Roll in Book 3,
- Flams in book 4,
- Flam 1/8th notes and Triplets in Book 5,
- Paradiddle in Book 6.

Before we move onto the next rudiment, we need to mention a fundamental or fundamentals we have covered within the Rudimentary sections of each of the first 6 books in the Time Space and Drums Series for very good reason.

With a few minor exceptions we are going to cover here in this book, these first five rudiments contain everything that all of the 40 plus rudiments include. By that I mean that there are really only single strokes, double strokes, and everything else is rooted in those two rudiments, single and double stroke rolls.

I said there are exceptions but mostly that is true, hence the reason for their inclusion here. I actually tried to not include them at all as the Time Space and Drums Series is about learning to play the drums and not learning the techniques involved.

But alas, I didn't win the argument as they are so vital and they are the drumming behind the drumming, so to speak. It is the science behind the science of drumming and so, try as I may, I couldn't get away with excluding them from the series. And mostly that is a good thing.

The Buzz Roll

So, on to the next rudiment: the buzz roll or the closed roll. By the way, the double stroke roll is often referred to as the open roll due to its more open sound when compared to the closed roll or buzz roll, whichever you prefer.

I simply refer to either as a roll and make an instantaneous decision as to which I play at any given time.

The buzz roll is created by striking the drum with the right-hand stroke and just letting the stick bounce on the drum head loosely. Then do the exact same thing with the left-hand. It is as simple as that.

However, the bounces need to be controlled and to help with this, you can begin by practicing 1/4 notes on the snare drum, along with a metronome at a slow speed and by playing alternate sticking. So, a single bar of 4/4 time would look something like this:

1, 2, 3, 4
R, L, R, L

But remember each right-hand and each left-hand are single strokes, followed by bounces of the stick on the snare drum.

So, taking the bounces into account, the above exercise would look something like this:

R RRR, L LLL, R RRR, L LLL

Keep in mind that the small R strokes and the small L strokes are not 1/16th notes. Although they may sound a little like sixteenths, they are simply loose, controlled bounces of the stick on the drum head or practice pad.

When you get the idea and begin to control the bounce of the stick on the snare drum, try doing the same playing 1/8th notes. It is important to remember that these are just exercises and the buzz roll is really played loosely and constantly throughout the bar. However, it is never really paying any attention to the pulse but, of course, you as the drummer are paying attention to the pulse; as such, you will begin and stop when the music you may be reading at any time informs you to stop. The buzz roll may just be for a single beat of the bar, 2 beats, 3 beats 4 or more beats and is a continued controlled bounce of the sticks.

So back to the exercise: eighth notes would look something like this:

1 & 2 & 3 & 4 &
R RRR, L LLL, R RRR, L LLL, R RRR, L LLL, R RRR, L LLL

When you have practiced this exercise, try the buzz roll by just bouncing one stick after the other and continuing the roll smoothly over an entire bar and more. Use a metronome as a guide and remember that you are really buzzing from right to left in a smooth fashion; you are buzzing to and fro and from right to left as the metronome clicks along; you listen to its click to stay in time and stay smooth.

Don't try to play 1/8th notes or any other note as these are simply bouncing of the stick from right to left. Another repetitive motion?

Featured Drummer Recommendations

Steve Gadd

Another drummer who is completely different in many ways from others is Steve Gadd. When I think about Steve Gadd, I am constantly drawn to the dynamics within his playing. You only have to watch the rhythm he created for Paul Simon's 50 Ways to Leave Your Lover which, on first hearing it, you may hear a rather quiet drum rhythm but when you really listen to it the dynamics are fantastic. It goes up and down in various places throughout the 2-bar phrase and that kind of playing is evident in just about everything Steve does.

A good example that shows the dynamics throughout a complete song is AJA by Steeley Dan.

Because we are specifically speaking about dynamics within a rhythm or song, what we are really referring to is the way something grooves. A groove is defined as *a long narrow cut or depression on the surface of a material.* Put another way, *a groove is an established route or habit.* In music and drumming specifically, we are speaking of *getting into a fixed routine or groove.* And Steve Gadd is known as the King of the groove.

In an earlier series, I made mention of Steve Smith and the flow he creates within his drumming which, although similar, is not quite the same as a groove. The groove is that special part of drumming that makes you want to tap your feet, referencing our innate recognition of repetitive sounds that we naturally want to move or dance to.

It goes without saying that any serious drummer should listen to quite a few Steve Gadd grooves. Doing so will help highlight the need for different sticking combinations and variations within any one beat because Steve plays every groove as if it was the most important thing within a piece of music.

The exercises within this Accents Foundation book are the groundwork for more advanced Steve Gadd type study. They allow the beginner to intermediate drummer to experience a variety of different drumming styles and possibilities, especially groove and dynamics.

Everything the drummer already knows will be enhanced and infused with increased dynamics and a better groove after some time of practicing the accent exercises within this book.

It, therefore, serves you to understand that the practice is not meant to result in brilliantly formed grooves as a cause in and of themselves. Better dynamic playing is the effect of the cause of practicing accent exercises which, like our Chad Wackerman notes on relaxation in the last book, clearly shows that speed is never the primary aim.

The primary aim is always precision and accuracy; therefore, it should always take precedence over speed and how fast you can play any particular exercise. The mind focused on the precision of dynamic accents will integrate with your playing to result in better dynamics within your drumming but, as suggested, this is an effect and not a cause.

Highly Recommended Listening

Within the Featured Drummer sections, so far, I have really refrained from recommending anything specific as far as possible. However, I highly recommend anything you can get from Steve Gadd's drumming, especially the following as there are prime examples of dynamic groove playing:

50 Ways To Leave Your Lover by Paul Simon.

AJA by Steeley Dan.

Chuckie's in Love by Ricky Leee Jones.

Plus anything else you can get featuring the groove merchant, Steve Gadd.

Conclusion

You should be absolutely sure that you have a firm mastery of the exercises in all of the books from 1-7 before moving on. This book, up to the end of book 8, should be perfected before going on to book 9, which deals with the more creative aspects of drumming.

Books 1-8 are really foundation courses in the skills involved in drumming and should be solid and smooth. Clear, crisp and tight. There should be no rattles or vibrations; everything should be tight.

Then go on to book 8. After which, more revision of the past parts of the series should be done before going on to book 9 through 12.

Meanwhile, enjoy.

Stephen J. Hawkins

Closing Note:
The Time Space and Drums series is intended as a complete program from Part 1 to Part 12. It is strongly advised that you follow the program in order of the parts as they integrate and build on each other. The only thing I can now add is to practice each exercise until you have them all mastered. Mastery comes from paying attention to the most basic fundamentals already covered in each of the exercises within this book.

Once you have perfected each exercise you may like to try them left-handed but that may take time depending on your current skill level.

Free Audio Demonstrations
Please don't forget to visit the following URL to download audio demonstrations of every exercise in this book as soon as possible. You will then receive soma additional tips and guidance through the included essence emails.

www.timespaceanddrums.com/tsd-7acc.html

What's Next

Thank you for choosing Time Space and Drums as one of your learning tools. I hope you enjoyed the process. You can explore more of the series in Discover Other Worlds, the eighth book in the series by searching for the "**Basic Latin Drumming Foundation**" at your favorite bookstore.

Share Your Experience

If you have a moment, please review this Rock Drumming Foundation book at the store where you bought it. Help other drummers and tell them why you enjoyed the book or what could be improved. Thank you!

Thank you again dear reader and I hope we meet again between the pages of another book. Remember, You rock!

Other Books by The Author

Modern Drumming Concepts
Rock Drumming Foundation Series part. (Six in-depth Drum Lessons).
Jazz Drumming Foundation Series part. (Six in-depth Drum Lessons).
Rock Drumming Development Series part. (Six in-depth Drum Lessons).
Jazz Drumming Development Series part. (Six in-depth Drum Lessons).
Odd Time Drumming Foundation Series part. (Six in-depth Drum Lessons).
Accents and Phrasing Series part. (Four in-depth Drum Lessons).
Basic Latin Drumming Foundation Series part. (Four in-depth Drum Lessons).

Have you ever thought about what it would feel like to make a living as a pro drummer?

If so, then visit the Drum Coach website. I might be for YOU!

The purpose of the Drum Coach blog is not only to provide drummers with valuable information but also to help them share their passions.

The Drum Coach provides all types of drumming information from beginner lessons right up to professional level playing skills, as well as personal self*(drummer)*-improvement essentials – there's something here no matter your skill level!

Some of the most important information on this website comes from my personal experiences as a percussionist and musician for over 35 years. So, I invite you to take advantage of the Drum Coach Experience, whose aim is to provide high-quality, on-demand information for drummers as they travel along their journey to achieve their personal drumming goals and ambitions.

Our commitment to our readers is always 100%! If you have any problems, questions, or concerns, just let us know and we'll help you take care of the situation as quickly as possible.

And remember to **Stay In Time!** and continue to **Rock!**

Printed in Poland
by Amazon Fulfillment
Poland Sp. z o.o., Wrocław